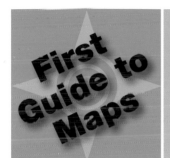

Mapping Your Community

Marta Segal Block and
Daniel R. Block

Heinemann Library
Chicago, IL

©2008 **Heinemann Library**
an imprint of Capstone Global Library, LLC
Chicago, Illinois

Customer Service 888-454-2279
Visit our website at **www.heinemannlibrary.com**

Designed by Jennifer Lacki, Kimberly R. Miracle, and Betsy Wernert

Illustrated by Mapping Specialists

Originated by Modern Age

Printed and bound in the United States of America, North Mankato, MN

14 13 12
10 9 8 7 6 5 4 3 2

10-digit ISBNs: 1-4329-0794-8 (hc); 1-4329-0800-6 (pb)

Library of Congress Cataloging-in-Publication Data

Block, Marta Segal.
Mapping your community / Marta Segal Block and Daniel R. Block.
    p. cm. -- (First guide to maps)
Includes bibliographical references and index.
ISBN-13: 978-1-4329-0794-5 (hc)
ISBN-13: 978-1-4329-0800-3 (pb)
1. Cartography--Juvenile literature. I. Block, Daniel, 1967- II. Title.
GA105.6.B56 2007
526--dc22

2007048624

Acknowledgments
The author and publishers are grateful to the following for permission to reproduce copyright
material: ©age footstock p. **26** (Jeff Greenberg); Alamy p. **18** (Dennis MacDonald); Corbis p.
17 (Will & Deni McIntyre); drr.net p. **27** (Dino Fracchia); Getty Images pp. **6** (Royalty Free), **7**
(Panoramic Images); Map Resources p. **4**; www.jasonhawkes.com p. **5**.

Cover image reproduced with permission of www.jasonhawkes.com.

062012
006755RP

Contents

Any words appearing in the text in bold, **like this**, are explained in the glossary.

What Are Maps?

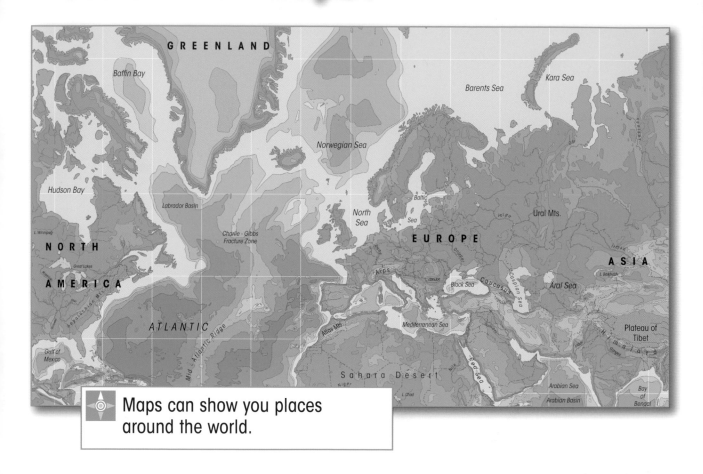

Maps can show you places around the world.

A map is a flat drawing of a part of the world. People who make maps are called **cartographers**.

You can use maps to learn about places far from where you live. You can also use them to learn about places close by.

Maps show places from a bird's eye view.

Mapping Your Community

A community is a group of people who have something in common. A community is a place where people might live, work, and play. There are big communities and small communities.

Your classroom and all the people in it are one community.

A city is a large community.

Your neighborhood is a small community. A city or town is a bigger community. It is part of another community, the state. The state is part of an even larger community, the country. Each community needs many maps.

Reading Maps

Maps have many features that help you read them.

Map title

Most maps have a **title**. A map title tells what information is on the map. For example, a map of a small town may list the town's name as the map title.

Compass rose

Many maps have a **compass rose**. This feature shows the **cardinal directions**. The cardinal directions are north, south, east, and west. North often points toward the top of the map.

Downtown Milton

Title

Residential area

Oak Street

School

Clinic

Post office

Main Street

Town hall

Library

Shops

Fire station

Walnut Street

Mill Street

North Street

Public park

Spring Street

Police station

First Street

View Street

N
W E
S

Compass rose

9

Map Symbols

Maps have many **symbols**. Symbols are small shapes and signs that represent objects in real life. For example, dots on a map may show cities. A star may show the **capital** of a state or country. The capital is the place where leaders of a country or state meet and work.

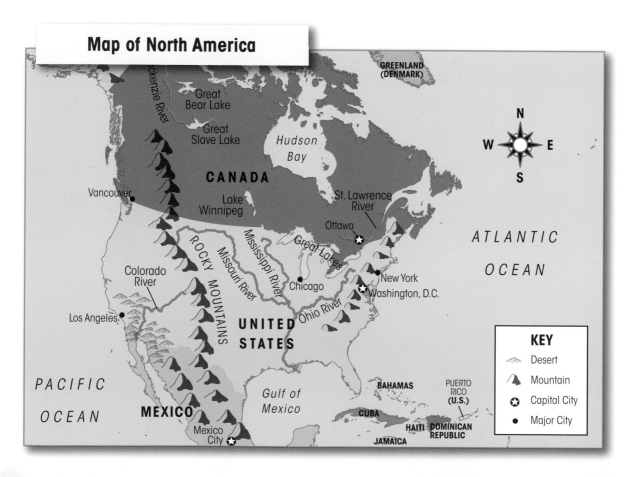

Map of North America

GREENLAND (DENMARK)

Mackenzie River

Great Bear Lake

Great Slave Lake

Hudson Bay

CANADA

Vancouver

Lake Winnipeg

St. Lawrence River

Ottawa

Great Lakes

ROCKY MOUNTAINS

Colorado River

Missouri River

Mississippi River

Chicago

New York

Washington, D.C.

Ohio River

Los Angeles

UNITED STATES

ATLANTIC OCEAN

N
W E
S

PACIFIC OCEAN

MEXICO

Gulf of Mexico

BAHAMAS

PUERTO RICO (U.S.)

Mexico City

CUBA

HAITI DOMINICAN REPUBLIC

JAMAICA

KEY
- Desert
- Mountain
- Capital City
- Major City

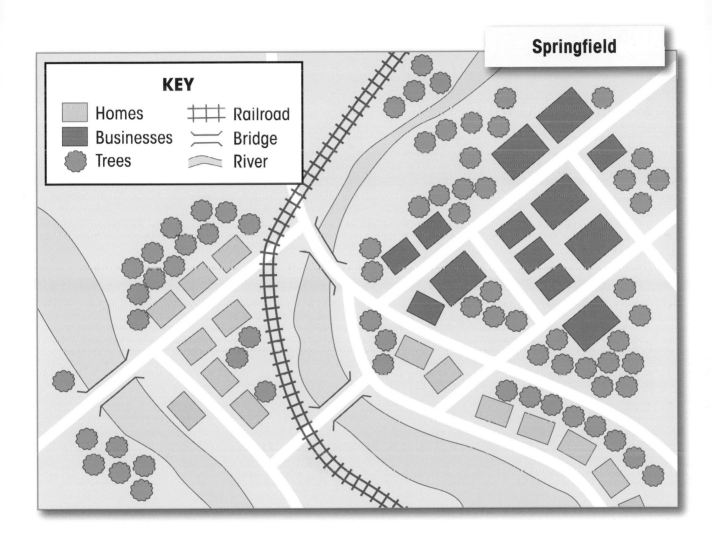

Springfield

KEY

Homes		Railroad	
Businesses		Bridge	
Trees		River	

Color is often used as a symbol on maps. On the map above, blue shows a river. White lines show roads.

Map key

Every map uses different colors and **symbols**. Maps have a **key** that tells what the colors and symbols mean. The key is a box that shows all the symbols on the map.

Scale

The **scale** is a feature that looks like a ruler. It can help you measure distance on a map. The scale shows how many miles or kilometers are represented by every inch or centimeter.

Look at the map on the next page. Can you use the scale to find the distance between the museum and Woodruff Park?

This is a map of Atlanta, Georgia.

KEY
- Building
- ◆ Place of Interest

Map key

Map scale

Fitting Things onto a Map

Europe

Maps must fit a large area onto a small surface. Some maps show very large areas, such as **continents**. These maps cannot show a lot of detail about a place. They may just show the location of the country.

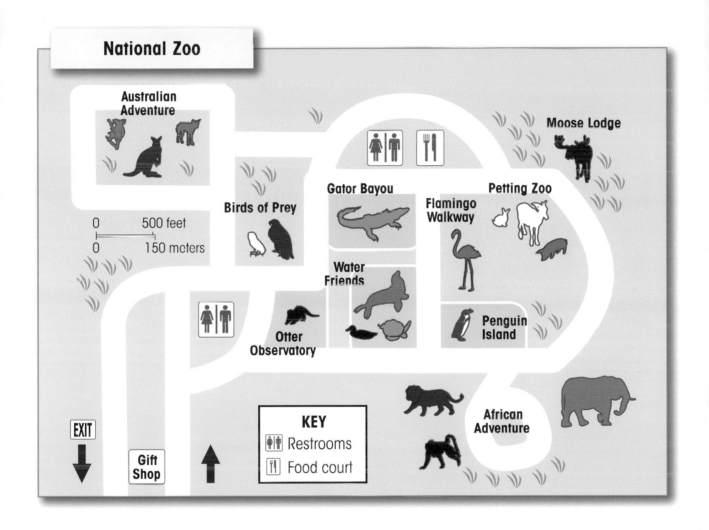

National Zoo

Australian Adventure

Birds of Prey

0   500 feet
0   150 meters

Gator Bayou

Water Friends

Otter Observatory

Flamingo Walkway

Moose Lodge

Petting Zoo

Penguin Island

African Adventure

EXIT

Gift Shop

KEY
👫 Restrooms
🍴 Food court

Other maps show smaller areas, such as cities or neighborhoods. They may just show one place, such as a museum or zoo. These maps show more detail than country maps. They may show streets, parks, and important buildings in the area.

Mapping Your Classroom

A map can show a community as small as your classroom. Teachers often make maps of their classrooms called seating charts. A seating chart shows the teacher who sits where and helps the teacher learn everyone's name.

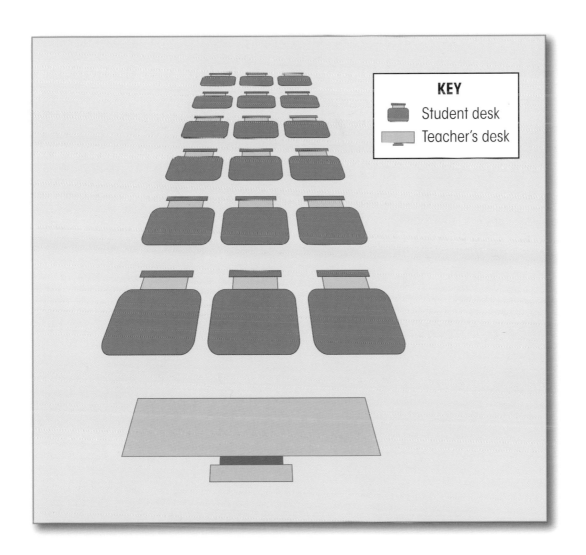

The map on this page shows a map of the classroom pictured at the left. It shows the location of each desk and shows where the teacher sits.

Mapping Your School

A map can show a larger community, such as a school. A school is bigger than a classroom. This means a map of a school would show less detail than a map of a classroom.

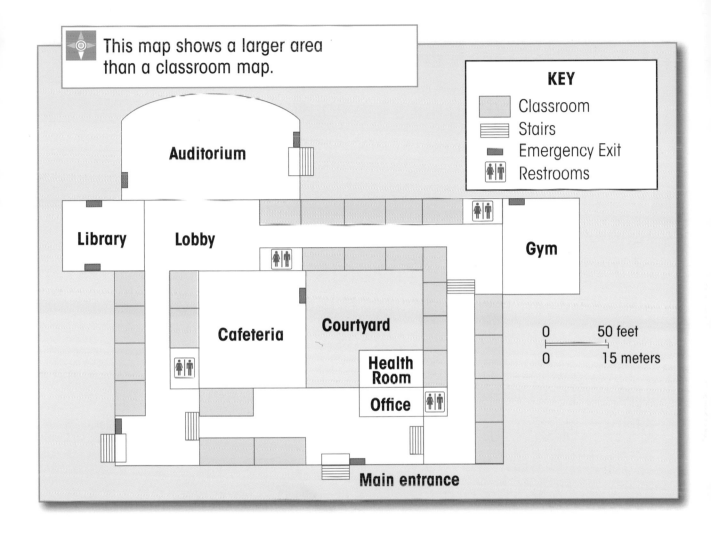

This map shows a larger area than a classroom map.

KEY
- Classroom
- Stairs
- Emergency Exit
- Restrooms

Auditorium

Library

Lobby

Gym

Cafeteria

Courtyard

Health Room

Office

0 — 50 feet
0 — 15 meters

Main entrance

A map of a school would show different information than a classroom map. The principal uses a school map to know the location of emergency exits and classrooms. The principal would not need a map with as much detail as a classroom map.

Mapping Your Neighborhood

A neighborhood includes the houses, apartment buildings, stores, parks, schools, and people in a small area.

A neighborhood map shows the location of some of these places. This is important information for someone who wants to start a business, buy a house, or learn more about the area.

The map on the next page shows the different places in a neighborhood. This map could be used to find the best way to travel from place to place. It shows a larger area than a map of a school, so the features are smaller.

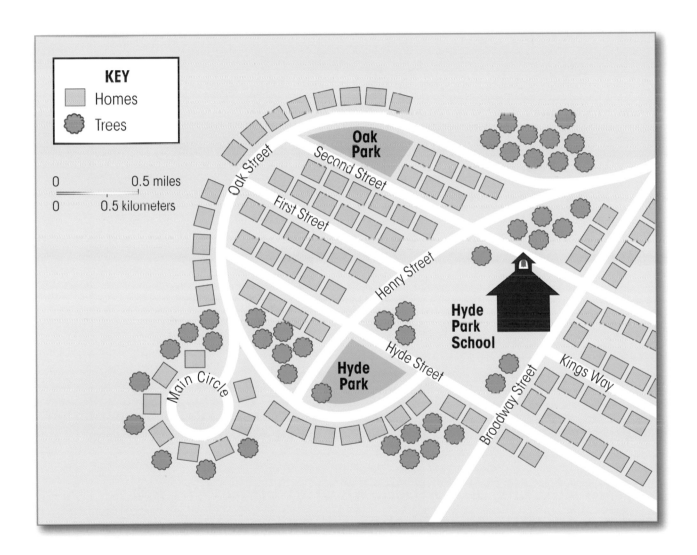

KEY
Homes
Trees

0   0.5 miles
0   0.5 kilometers

Oak Street
Second Street
Oak Park
First Street
Henry Street
Hyde Street
Hyde Park
Main Circle
Hyde Park School
Broadway Street
Kings Way

Mapping Your City or Town

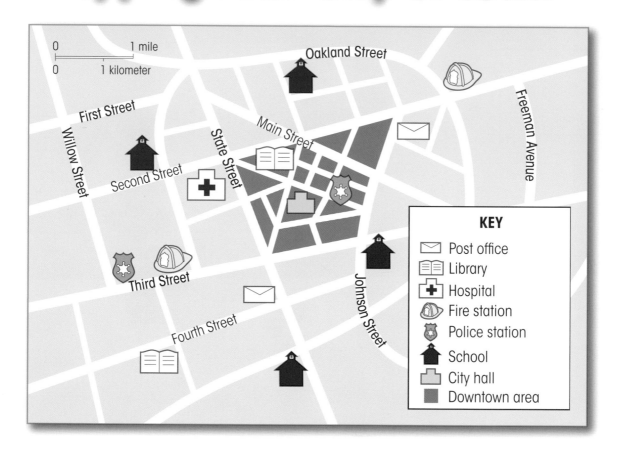

A map of a city or town shows an even larger area than a neighborhood. It shows the location of important buildings, parks, and streets. The features on a city or town map are even smaller than the features on a neighborhood map.

People who manage cities and towns need many maps. Firefighters need a map that shows the location of **fire hydrants**. If a pipe needs to be repaired, city workers need a map of the water pipes beneath the street.

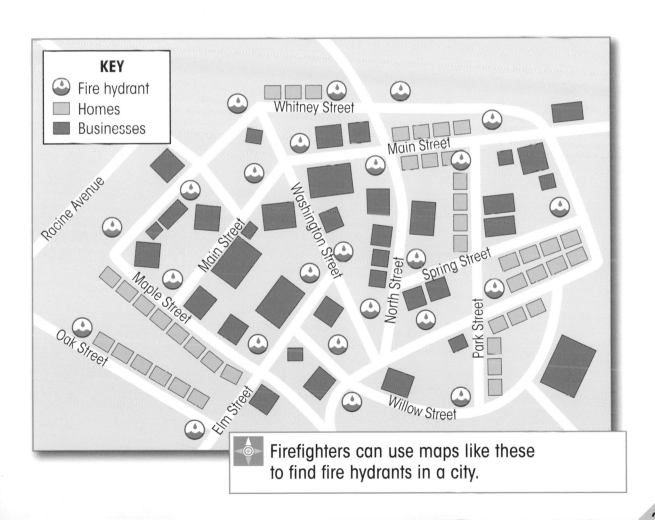

KEY
- Fire hydrant
- Homes
- Businesses

Whitney Street
Main Street
Racine Avenue
Main Street
Washington Street
North Street
Spring Street
Park Street
Maple Street
Oak Street
Elm Street
Willow Street

Firefighters can use maps like these to find fire hydrants in a city.

Mapping Your State and Country

Maps can show a very large community, such as a state or country. A state map includes few details. It may show large cities, mountains, rivers, or lakes.

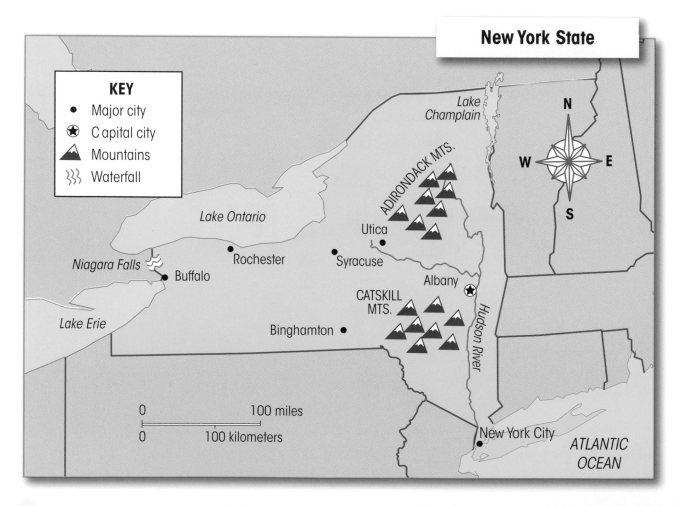

New York State

KEY
- Major city
- ⊛ Capital city
- ▲ Mountains
- 〰 Waterfall

Lake Champlain

ADIRONDACK MTS.

Lake Ontario

Utica

Niagara Falls

Rochester

Syracuse

Buffalo

Albany ⊛

CATSKILL MTS.

Lake Erie

Binghamton

Hudson River

N
W   E
S

New York City

ATLANTIC OCEAN

0   100 miles

0   100 kilometers

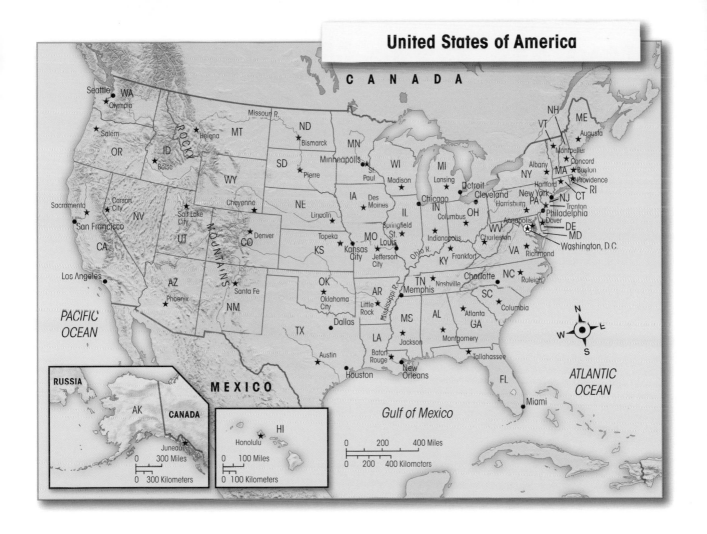

A country map must fit an even larger area of land onto a map. It may only show a few major cities, the **capital** of each state and the country, and the **borders** between states. It may also show large bodies of water and mountains.

How Are Maps Made?

In order to make maps, people first need to collect the information for an area. Cities and towns hire people called **surveyors**. Surveyors carefully measure the location of streets, firehydrants, and pipes in an area. They record the information to help **cartographers** prepare a map.

Surveyors use special tools to measure the land.

Cartographers can create maps on computers.

Surveyors and cartographers can use photographs taken from an airplane to help them make maps. Surveyors also use photographs taken by **satellites** from space.

Together, surveyors and cartographers map the communities around us. We use this information to learn more about places all over the world.

Map Activities

Activity 1: Map Your Classroom

Imagine a new student is joining your class. Make a map of the classroom for this new student. You cannot show everything on your map, so think about what kind of information he or she will need to know. Don't forget to include features like a **title** and **key**.

Activity 2: Map Your Street

1. Think of a situation where someone would want a map of your street. Maybe a new family is moving to the block. Maybe the fire department wants a map in case there's a fire.

2. Make a list of the things your map will need to show.

3. Draw your map. Don't forget to include features like a **compass rose**, **scale**, and key.

How would your map be different if it was of the whole neighborhood?

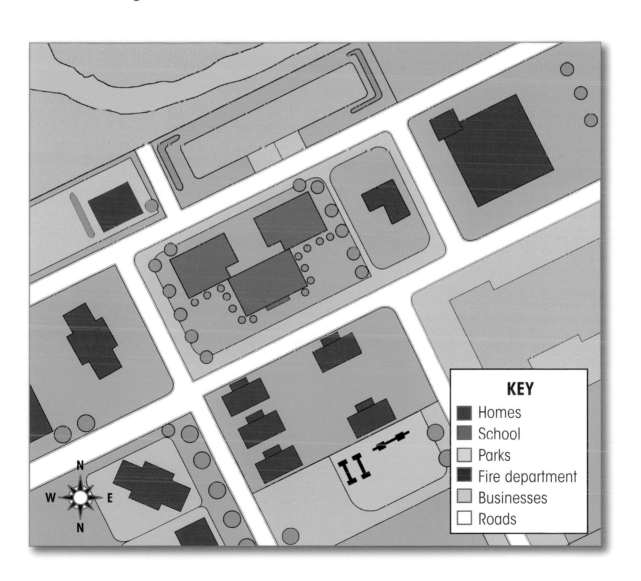

KEY
- Homes
- School
- Parks
- Fire department
- Businesses
- Roads

Glossary

border imaginary line that divides two places

captial city where leaders of a state or country meet and work

cardinal direction one of the four main directions: north, south, east, or west

cartographer person who makes maps

compass rose symbol on a map that shows direction

continent very large area of land surrounded by water; there are seven continents in the world.

fire hydrant water pipe above the ground that firefighters connect a hose to

key table that shows what the symbols on the map mean

satellite object that travels above Earth and sends information back to Earth

scale tool on a map that can be used to measure distance

surveyor person who makes measurements of the land

symbol picture that stands for something else

title feature that tells what you will find on a map

Find Out More

Organizations and Websites

The Websites below may have some advertisements on them. Ask an adult to look at them with you. You should never give out personal information, including your name and address, without talking to a trusted adult.

American Automobile Association (AAA)
AAA (called "Triple A") is a group of related automobile clubs. AAA clubs provide free map and direction services to members. Visit **www.aaa.com** to find a AAA club near you, or put AAA and your state name into a trusted search engine.

National Geographic
National Geographic provides free maps and photos of Earth. They also have articles about people and animals. Visit **www.nationalgeographic.com**.

Yahoo Maps
Find directions from your house to places nearby and far away. Try putting in your address and the address of your school. Do the directions given match your route? Visit **www.maps.yahoo.com**.

Books to Read

Baber, Maxwell. *Map Basics*. Chicago: Heinemann Library, 2006.

Holub, Joan. *Geogra-Fleas: Riddles All Over the Map*. Morton Grove, IL: Albert Whitman & Company, 2004.

Bredeson, Carmen. *Looking at Maps and Globes*. New York: Children's Press, 2001.

Index